destination out

destination out

poems by charles c smith

TIGHTROPE BOOKS

Copyright © charles c. smith, 2018

All rights reserved. No part of this publication may be reproduced, stored in a retrieval system, or transmitted, in any form or by any means, without prior permission of the publisher or, in the case of photocopying or other reprographic copying, a licence from Access Copyright, the Canadian Copyright Licensing Agency. www.accesscopyright.ca, info@accesscopyright.ca. Printed in Canada.

Tightrope Books
#207-2 College Street,
Toronto Ontario, Canada M5G 1K3
tightropebooks.com
bookinfo@tightropebooks.com

EDITOR: Jim Nason
COPYEDITOR: Deanna Janovski
COVER DESIGN: David Jang
COVER PHOTO: Piron Guillaume
LAYOUT DESIGN: David Jang

Produced with the assistance of the Canada Council for the Arts and the Ontario Arts Council.

Library and Archives Canada Cataloguing in Publication

Smith, Charles C., 1953-, author
    Destination out / Charles C. Smith.

Poems.
ISBN 978-1-988040-39-4 (softcover)

    I. Title.

PS8637.M5595D48 2018   C811'.6   C2018-900858-X

*... your body is full of ears
listen to it ...*

*... the only thing i hear
is your heart ...*

for bia

Praise for *destination out*

"In *destination out*, smith takes the reader on a lyrical, poetic hang-time experience roller coasting through the vastly deep infinite skies between childhood adventures, an estranged father, and a wayward young man's rebirth, redemption, and adult-awakened confidence rooted in jumping, life-breathing jazz. smith is highly skilled at his craft and often insightfully contemplative. The reader becomes mindful 'in the cool air, in the morning. silence, on the streets, the death of passing. a warm light slants on the church steps, across the way, a brilliant emptiness.' smith pivots and nails spectacular turnaround jump shots conjuring jazz greats: Jelly Roll Morton, Josephine Baker, Bud Powell, and other improvisational luminaries. This is more than imitation ragtime wolverine blues. These poems are tight, meticulously crafted, syncopated, and always invoking meaningful light. *destination out* is a true revelation and a must read!" —Michael Fraser, author of *To Greet Yourself Arriving*

"charles c. smith is a true poet: not only an artisan of rhythm and words, but a conjurer of the quiet voices who reside in liminal space. We hear in his works the pain of injustice and loss, the tragedies of the marginalized and near-forgotten, and the hope of redeeming history. Smith jars the reader out of the comfort zones of the warm and familiar and into the places that disquiet our hearts and minds. *destination out* is a brave work." —Dr. Georgia Wilder, lecturer/writing instructor, New College, University of Toronto

"charles c. smith's poetry is about walking 'out of circumstance' by people who know 'first-hand / all the patterns of the darkness.' It has the urgency of breath and the beauty of blood. The speaker in these poems recounts the journey of his family through time in a voice 'deep as death.' Smith's poetic language is a fractured mirror held up to stories, defying the limits of observation." —Bänoo Zan, author of *Songs of Exile*

CONTENTS

a piece of twisted steel

another life	13
atavism	14
between destinies	15
birth right	17
recanting visions	18
doors and exits	20
trinity	21
your presence, absence and sudden death	22
links	24
daydreaming about my father	26
the bedroom	28
spaces and distances	29
a window shattering into light	30
poem that needs no title	33
bookends	35
after the years	40

destination out

after the rain	42
night at the opera	44
the natural-born gambler	45
jelly roll	47
dinner at frenchman's	48
awakening	49
jazz cleopatra/black venus	51
grievance	55

tea for two	56
last song?	60
destination out	61
another part	65
journeying	66
the end of things	67

an empty foxhole filled with fiddleheads

wednesday	70
sunday evening	71
this troubled garden	72
a piece of twisted steel	73
circumstance	74
pérdida	75
abuelita enters	77
planting the seeds	78
conflict	79
rape	80
ghost woman	82
the goddess	84
the goddess dance	85
lilia's dance	87
vision of the seen	89
hindsight	90
mary	91
to listen without light	93
the order of things	94
the passing of light	95

discretion	97
stillness	98
weekend spaces	99
retribution	100
at the edge	101
whispers	102
decisions	103
a place to be	104
this thing called time	105
first snow	106
distance	107
letting go	108
aknowledgements	110
about the author	112

a piece of twisted
steel

another life

in an old house on staten
island, it seems another life
with chipped green tiles

on the back and sides of the roof
and grey front porch stairs
bending to even the slightest step—

i could crack one, easily
a simple jump would do, then fall
into a dark cluttered basement

its low ceiling and large holes
seemingly full of rats
the smell of dried earth, and rags—

and between dim light and dampness
in a hallway grinning without teeth

i swore to things i could not see
to fear and wonder and cat's eyes
like yellow embers in unenviable dark—

to death and the bodies of siblings
and strangers, lying on the floor
in places where i could not see them

all of them, now in my dreams
like schoolchildren on halloween
without make-up, in the graveyard

of an abandoned church, its steeple
veiled in fog, beside cracked white
gravestones, wide-eyed hysterical

and waiting waiting waiting   to go home

atavism

wind moves   against ocean
gulls cry beach sand swirls
i thought i would be drowned
by the waves i never could swim
and have never lost fear
of the floor below green water
its shifts or sudden
disappearance

a paradigm of living
i do not like cannot take
without thought of those
who never come back
but find their place
among the seaweed and the shells
somewhere under in a watery
room   provided for burial
the lost body   making its way
without light without comfort
of a blanket to make the flesh dry

my brother liked the ocean
so went under to the houses
kept neat and hidden in green dark
my father named me after him
at times i have his yearnings
and when cool water rushes
at my back i feel a gentle
undertow sucking, sucking

between destinies

there are times   i wonder what it must have been like
for you   with me inside a full six months and kicking
and him outside   lying flat and still
in a casket   open for two days in a funeral parlour

other times   i think of you spending your night
looking out the bedroom window   into a sky
full of dark promises   and small lights you hoped
he would pass by   so that you could see him
as he would always be   an angel fading into space

and when they laid him   in a boxed parcel
into the gaping   sun-dried earth
you must have felt   torn as no other
between destinies   with a small heart
at work in your womb   and the gentle brown
eyes of a young boy   closed forever

semblances of your pain   must have appeared to you
and i could see you   seeing yourself with
an arm cut off   the blood bursting into a pool
or standing in a field   of fading green
as the earth opened up   below your feet
to suck you in   like a puddle

i was always told   it took six men
to drag you   from that burial
kicking and screaming   how badly you wanted
in   while the earth fell on him like a ton

later you told me   this was something
you would never recover from   and that
your heart beats   like a barking dog
each year   on the day of his death

then you swear   there are moments when
you see him again   thru me
as if he had walked   out of circumstance
into my body   so that when i stand
in front of you   you see a part of him

the earth just could not   swallow

birth right
for charles

to me   you will always be
a face with my features   your eyes
open peepholes   with brown pebbles

lips   thin and moist and red
your skin so clear   a creamy
brown   complexion

you held a fixed gaze   staring
out   from an eleven-by-fourteen
shimmering   black metallic

picture frame   in the hallway
outside the living room   beneath
a blue night light   no one ever used

and supported   by a small nail
from that height   of perpetuity
you looked down   on everything

in front of a wall behind which i thought
the mystery   of your disappearance had been
buried like a cure-all   in a medicine chest

and each day   i greeted you
almost as if i were   greeting myself
as someone   who knew first-hand

all the patterns   of the darkness you
followed   after slipping under the
white crests   of an afternoon's lazy waves

only to surface   months later on the wall
the centre of the family   with a set smile
your reply   to anything

my face full of wonder   fearful
of the knowledge   of my given name

recanting visions

light between buildings burns
the leaves and ivy that cling
in precise patterns above
curbside near a deserted park—

you walked there
a notepad and pen full of hauntings
you wanted out thru telling
whomever would listen
what you knew you did not do
on that day you spent suspect of death—

—which happened   in a green cloud
twisted spitting waves   with your
back turned to wind and surf
and blinding afternoon sunlight
spread across a beach where he slipped
beneath cool waters quietly away—

and in that moment   you were
carried alone   in calm water
trembling in silence   and absolute fear
certain you were not   seeing
what there could only be to see
after being   seduced to swim
while at your back   a boy
floated under the shade
silent waters conceal

ii
and so between my given name
and your reaction to it   what else could
there be?   you saw choked
white waves   cloudless skies
where he ran on sand
as you dove into the cross breeze—

i recalled a single black-and-white photo
a boy in a bright white nightshirt   and a faint smile
hung on the living room wall   quiet and holy—

one violated memory like a hallucinogen
the other was decorated in shadow
both a brutality   fixing who we were to them
for looking once and then again
and still not to see him   swallowed up by august heat
and the rising waters of an empty beach—

years later   you added up knockouts
in the corner of a ring   led protests
spoke revolution   bandaged paper
to your thought and skin—

i left that space   of stubborn tongues
and wrapped fists   of words crushed by hunger
bleeding into night   only to find again
to leave behind   that lost boy
choked by seaweed   and crab shells
sand dollars   and sharp stones
and the songs of leaves   in surrounding
beachside trees plunged into grief—

and for years   we wandered
these worlds   bones broken in memory
floating as if in a medicated space
within a spiral   of endless night ...

doors and exits

in the cool air, in the morning. silence, on the streets, the death of
passing. a warm light slants on the church steps, across the way,
a brilliant emptiness. stones, a light grey space, a door hammered, out
of the wrought iron of poverty, to glow like a shadow of gold.
in an isolated place, the provisions for those who do not want to live,
in desolation.

trinity

my father   was an oxford man
(so my mother tells me)   and at times i relate
my own education   to this renowned platitude

but there is   little
my father and i   have in common here
he sucked in knowledge   from a privileged
source   while i put my lips
up to the hems   of priesthood

this was certainly   a barrier
scholars and theologians have never mixed
(except over martinis)   and i hardly
knew my father   nor he me
when i was four   death offered
him   a course of study
my mother says   he wanted
badly

now he has it
and i have   my mother
and together we are
the remaining edges of a
strange   trinity

your presence, absence and sudden death

when you became weary
arms heavy,
bones aching
of touch and taste, sight
and smell
and journeying thru many states and cities
you sat down on the old grey porch
on a green lawn chair
beside window boxes full of flowers
and stared
into the 1957 black asphalt streets
of staten island, morning star road, father of one of the few
black families living amongst portuguese, irish, italian, polish
working-class whites

it was summer
and i was three
and excited to see you
after what seemed so long a time
i was laughing,
jumping on my heels
even tho there were those
who wanted to protect you from me
as if a laughing child could bring on death
(but you wanted
nothing of this, bade
them let me see you, tried
to rise
and push them out of the way
then fell, slowly
back in your chair
as they whisked your will away)
i could only
hug you, briefly
and stare at you from the distance of
the front door, at the top of the grey stairs, with hope

rising in my throat like a small blue bird, wanting to
escape into your arms, into the warmth of memories
delicate as an antique quilt

then i remember sunlight, falling
wave after wave, onto what
appeared on a screen
for a silent charlie chaplin
running down streets
splotched with light—the first miles
journeying into what seemed
your strangely quiet death

links

after a while   i begin
to think of him   as something
more than human   larger
than thought   a source
for emotions   i must now
in dawn-glow   rationalize

he was like   a salesman
at my door   a light knock
mumbled sentences   the black
briefcase opening   closing
then a doorknob   clicking
into lock   so that i never
learned much   about him
beyond old photos   or stories
of siblings whose lines
have changed   with each telling
they created   new passages for him
between nassau miami chicago
toronto new york where it all ended
on staten island   a place still
draped in confederate grey   italian
irish   red black and green
his gravestone   a small square slab
set in a churchyard   remote
as any   obscurity

now i piece together what i can
with litmus paper   probe and test
the tales told   photos taken
against a mental profile
of black men   their
thirst   for drugs and alcohol
or other things   that total up
to failure   and misery

and this is where i find him
at times   on a corner of some
city   sitting amongst dog ends
piles of trash   enduring the cheapness
of brown bags   tossed off
cigarets   and quarters
from the hands of white men
who ask that he sing
"mammy"   one more time

daydreaming about my father

a red patch of earth   comes out
of nowhere   leads
to nothing

at its centre   a tree
stranger to such open land
where only   sky
and cloud   convene

elsewise   patches of daisies
forsythia   lilies
yellow and white heads
answerable   to whatever rains

answerable to the slow
tight circle   of birds
that have returned
to their summer   homes

i imagine you   resting
in this   place
far from   the motions
of either   of our lives

you are not   like your-
self   you are
now a quiet man   and the rose
you wear   like a medal
is the signal   you give me

to enter this precious kingdom

and i do   and you speak
and i hear within this silence
how you   like a sad boy have grown
away   from your past

the black filing cabinets   endless
telephone calls   and deadlines deadlines deadlines
dragging you down
into the grave   you did
not regret

i imagine you   now
as you would   likely see me
a man with an open
wound the size   of a fist
inexplicably held to a position
despite the cap and gown
of accumulated years   of intelligence

the only difference is   i move
out of the footprints you made
long ago   more knowledgeable
of the place   you now occupy

and this   you must realize
is my growth   thru years
of understanding   you
who could never comprehend
the significance   of being called
nigger

the bedroom

you closed the door   when it wasn't needed
you painted it white   as a bride gown

and placed in the centre   a thin black cross
to muffle the sounds of a man   whose moaning

kept you awake   those nights dark agonies
you wanted   kept secret as legend

the brown chair   bedside tables and other furnishings
you left as he liked them   like icons in a sacred place

with the curtain pulled back   in the afternoon
on the left side as you always did so he could see

sitting up in bed   his children playing ball
in the backyard   their years of being fathered

fading as a yellow jacket   in the summer breeze

with his trousers pressed and folded   over the back
of a black chair   his white shirts hanging in
the open closet   as if clouds caught in short sleeves

you made sure all things   were routinely placed
with soft brown slippers   waiting patiently by the side
of the bed   for feet that did not move at all

this is what you wanted of him   keepsakes
neatly arranged   like ornaments in a jewellery box
you refused to open   even tho you could not lock away

memories of his body   tossing in pain
until a final spasm left him   stiff as a spoon

on an operating table   flooded with light

spaces and distances

there are days, you can walk as far as you like. into death, memory. into green leaves hanging, like closed curtains, over the earth. covering the mouth, of what you can, recall. voices in a certain space, blue and yellow and shaped, by a small boy who stood on a precipice, of melting steel. then there were sounds, breaths in the dead air. clouds like sailors, over the clause of speech, the only possible escape. you are there, as you must be, a guardian of images, who will only talk, with you. a failure of brilliance.

a window shattering into light

so many days you had spent   arguing allegory
your words moved where they would   you followed

this line of reason   pathway to a castle
the throne concealed   in yellow light   a paradise

you argued the existence   of heaven
thought sometimes of a man   you swore you put him there

with nights of prayer   so many other gifts coming after
you threw out the line   he tied it tight

you would not move   a muscle of belief
and when you were
                                          alone
he dreamed
                    coming back to you
one evening when stars   bright old birds abandoned
their old   heights

he wanted   pure as sapphire among them
to tell you something
                              was eager as birth
so he returned to you
                              (an orange crown on the floor
fluorescent paint   a perfect circle
each point on it a thin pyramid   lines
with sharp edges   you wanted to cut yourself
and watch the blood   flood the crown
baptize   a king)

*

before this circle glow   presence
of infinity   you sat
alone   where you always
this perfect unearthliness
appearing   an equation
at your feet   without voice
or equal sign   not recognizable
as symbols of water   air
the terrible strain
of breath
                    putting the tea
kettle to boil   on a stove you set
two cups   you always did
and he visited   without flesh
and you lapsed   a delphic
into coma   memory
and he   without a word
demanded   you speak

later you said it was difficult to accept this
vision of a guest on polished white floor tiles
assembled pieces a crown at the foot of the table
you were amazed it pierced thru the storm window
silent as frost in the early light of spring
and you were sure you heard music a coronation
trumpets drums fanfare of hands voices in hosanna
you were certain you felt the floor
lift beneath you a kite in a breeze
the house suspended upon nothingness
the neon crown monocle of deity staring up
you acknowledged receipt of a message
his words from some far-off not attainable in the flesh

*

    the morning after   when dim
    light parted curtains   with a finger of sun
    you revealed
                       this silence   your heart skipped beats
    and there were words   mysteries with coffee
    toast brown sugar butter
                       sliding
    into place   you wove your experience
    as at a loom
                 the yarn threaded theory
    clothed spirit   you didn't want anyone to explain
    your anxiety
               that sudden weakness of gravity
                               your faith
    so you told us
                there was a voice
    from some forest   deep as death
    you told us there was a face   like a
    firefly at the window
                vanishing into night
    you told us there was   darkness
    a soul   condemned to wander 'til deliverance
    you told us there was   a crown
    on the waxed floor
                 a choir of angels somehow words
    without sound   let you know
    there is an end to suffering   and he found
    space   inside the gates   heaven

poem that needs no title

one day they will heap
dirt on you. you will lie,
eyes closed, peeking into
that ultimate night.

white lilies on the black
coffin in which you rest,
red and pink roses placed
on the polished casket's sides,

what you will see is debatable.
perhaps cinema darkness
before the spectrum of film

or the lustrous pitch of coal
that colours the last exhibit
behind horror house doors.

or, perhaps, you will see emptiness
and your soul, that fragile
whisper, will crawl into
the corners of the flesh
seeking blood flow, corpuscles,
breath—unwilling, finally,
after much speculation, to crawl
into that certain uncertainty.

but the dirt, still, will fall.
at first, a gentle shower
from hands that were
once close to you.
then, deluge follows
from the shovels of grumbling
men you never knew.

what happens next is untranslatable.
you will be a voice, perhaps
sentient, without a tongue
forever hovering about the borders
of the world
ignorant, as always,
of the power of speech.

bookends
for edmund and momma

the beauty of the sky—new york
in october, nassau in may—

reds, oranges, yellows
against an endless blue
dotted with seagull and cloud—

i fly in a small jet at the last
moment—this flight into what i learned

set off   by a voice   long distance
caught on call display—

area code   and message
covering a seemingly   impassable space

where the polite stammered greeting
foretells   your demise—

and so, dear brother, dear mother
we now have both—each gone
before i was ready to say goodbye

you picked up like night club patrons
bored at the end of a tab

even tho i thought   one would chase
that day away with a hedge stick   and the other
outwit and outrun   that inevitable ghost—

but when it was your time   you coughed
prayers through muted tongues

in the dry air   of a shared hospital room
divided by curtains   pale yellow walls

paint chips on the floor   and leaves
brushed against windows   like drums
beating light   into shade—

ii
then to see you   sitting in a partially upright bed
withered and thin   aware of your time

tubed   rosary nostrils and veins
dry arms   and shadow

bones   flesh pressed
each joint so brittle   the sweat on your forehead

you fell so witting into madness
and a remorseful   anguished silence

jaundice   a yellow fire in your eyes—

iii
(for edmund)

and each day   in that last week

shortly after dawn   i sat
beside you   listening to machines—

heart rate and blood pressure   breath and brain waves
rain against windows   nurses came and went

it seemed almost every thirty minutes   someone
recorded your vitals

then looked at you   with longing and a slight sigh—

a young tall doctor   (possibly his first passing)
upping and lowering your dose

no longer   waiting for your reply

he sees you with that   smile that sees
between what is caught   in the faint vestibule of light—

you both knew   what would happen
there was only so much   even the cancer could bear

the gradual   shutting of each part of you

so that dull air pushed in
as if it were   a thousand tons—

iv
"as above
so below"   (but is it the same for outside and in?)

deep lines across your faces   eyes sunken
brown stones

cheeks veins shrunken   your neck
and all your bones   threatened to break free—

one   sleeping into conspiracy
seeing her undoing   at the hands of one of her sons—

the other at a phone   fingers struggling
to call the district attorney   to release
his daughter   he dreamed he put in custody—

one   fists clenched against
the murder   hidden in his hair—

the other   waking to the pain he felt
he would leave behind   randomly assigned—

v
(for momma)

spring light sliced   the wall on the other
side of your bed where you lay almost asleep

mid-afternoon   one of my visits
a bible on the blanket   above your chest

you asked for psalms   and that i read them
slowly while you slept   perhaps so you could dream

the priest you once thought   you had for a moment like this
in the room   fully robed with eucharist and oil

the words fell from my lips   in whispers
dancing on that small smile   your deepening wound—

there was such silence then   between words
hushed and simple   hovering in air

your wanderings on the other side
a whirl of syllables   measuring last breaths—

vi
what if anything did either of you see when you woke—
(if you woke   and if there were such a thing as waking?)—

i barely recall   my last sight of night before sleep—

was this anything like   what you entered
without any possibility   of return?

were there words feelings   thoughts you
moved in   more diaphanous than flesh?

what music, if any   captured your now freed soul?

vii
and then   there was what would be done with what remained—

it had been quite some time   since either last ate
so there was so much less   to depart—

what you were to wear   was so much more
than what you had   become

you were made up thinner   powdered brown
your last wraps taken in

your eyes and cheeks ashen
your coffin opened   at service
and only closed before entering the hearse—

what you were leaving   was not very certain
where you were going   left even less to describe—

neither you nor we could see   all you had to do
to find what stays   beyond telling

and with flesh no longer an obstacle   you were suddenly gone

and we   for the first time could not follow—

after the years

i have lost the trees in the light. the orange glow on leaves a slow and tender falling, evening in this deceitful place, this chaotic and bothersome entrance. into love, the horizon stretched, across memory. the winter walk down a mile-long street, to kneel in blazing dark, with voices made of wind. then memory becomes a chalice, in the rooms of light, holding the challenge of mourning. until silent wings fell on the day, a sudden blow, full of simple wonderings

destination out

i don't want to know "how one does it," because i know too well and i don't want to know how the fire is retained ... ironically enough i want to know the exact opposite of these ... how to guard oneself against the intensity of one's own vision.

gwendolyn macewen

after the rain

lightning slashes a darkening sky
that falls into severed stones
of stars and a sliced moon
that hang like fireflies—

clouds splinter into prisms here
inside the lines of a late august sunset
like an hour glass emptying crystal
a bone washed in blinding sand
or some other thing veiled in infancy—

then rain fell sweeping sheets
on streets and sidewalks
stray dogs and lamp posts
windows and tree limbs
and thin leaves girded against assault

dangling in front of cracked white windowsills
where street signs and house lights
rattled electric lines like chains

raccoons racing rooftops and fence posts
squalling and chattering their teeth—

ii
and in all of this it was clear
what the day's stretch surrendered—

a blaze in the eyes
each trajectory balanced like shadow

and that long cadence of something unusual
caught up in the tongue of fear—

what was left had gone without notice
every greeting without hands—

no one knew anymore the order of destruction
such outrageous destitution evident on every street—

and then to see it all wrapped up in ads
on the walls of subways shelters and death row—

iii
what happens in the corners stays there
vision is limited at dusk by supply

the overt circumstances of disorder
breathe like spiders on newly spun webs—

winds hang in catastrophe
gutters flooded with emotion

synchronicity sat at the very heart of this distress

and somewhere woven into the distance of trees
a symbol of suffering swings like a rope—

iv
still the rains fell
a persuasive percussion pounding

and the scent that rose up in its wake
hovered over the lips of those who dare not speak—

night at the opera

how the first and final curtain rose
and fell as usual for this sort of pageant

set in ads local and state-wide
a performance in the moment

white linen passed through black doors
and were seated orderly by fee to be

up front in that last applause
hands in anticipated appreciation

all patrons given somewhat the same
six or four or two shells between boxes and balcony

children and ladies sitting in the hallways and aisles

a man spread-legged and his back full of trees
tied to a hoisted mast his insides streaming

after a procession down the town's main square
through the back door green room up wings and stairs

to whistles cat-calls-row-rattling-stomping feet
until all bullets were done and the body

in countless red slabs
lay under flood lights on the polished black floor ...

the natural-born gambler
for bert williams

the funniest man i ever saw—and the saddest man i ever knew.
                                                                w.c. fields

and did the black paint on your brown face mean
so much to those who caught you in their gaze?

with that mark across your cheeks and sable coat
top hat spats cane bow tie and dark eyes

in a bleached white shirt singing coon to dahomey
behind that self-made toothy grin

jitterbugging streets and alleys
the circuit almost always the same

on your own in the mist of this fury
pressing through burnt bones and fields

what dangled from a tree and lit a horizon
setting bodies into a flurry of smoke and steam

you countered with gambler abyssinia nobody
ziegfeld recordings and bandana land

where some walked from the lights you
set behind velvet curtains cut in gold trim

with laughter and tears the scalding of skin
and you now getting it in every way

a bahamian in the mix of dollars and lynch mobs
alone outside or inside a tavern standing still

as if hot tar wore you cheeks and cravat
your gloves bleeding grief from a blade

that cut you inside more than out
until you snapped into anger like its twin

pretending to pretend to be something to please a crowd
clouding contempt on stage screen bars barns

and fishing upstream
you took what they set to show them themselves through you

masked in devices of the shifty lazy and dumb
your gaze tarred them silhouettes and shadows

in that bottomless spate of hate
where they traced you from old shylock to years after

when the navy crowned a ship in your name
you would not in your time have been able to board ...

jelly roll

one day a brown box filled with horns
welcomed you home you had been so far
lips and hips taken this way then another
twisted into something less purposeful
the morbidity of your transient hue—

black mask and light brown cheeks
claiming distant memories
you set out distractions
your fingers astride a piano
mascara drying tarred skin—

small wonder you bit satire like a bone
with bleating goat car horns and laughter
to give you some sense of place
in a space that was not home—

then when you played and after
not many had anything to offer
aside from what you laid down they knew
you were king minstrel slick jive and jabber

each note every inch your conceit
in that almost passable space
between what you were and what
you knew you could never be

so hid your sound in barnyard bells
the comedienne in a face you did not own
trombones banjos trumpets and drums
bottles popping tables and dance floors

you took to your own under a wide-brimmed
straw hat three-piece linen suit and bow tie
on stage beneath balconies and street lamps
black-faced in new orleans—

dinner at frenchman's

and were you there
the night jelly bounced keys
like a ball in his hands?

no doubt dinner was stingy—
beer steak and soft potatoes
because no one came to eat

but to watch jelly's fingers pick keys
as he would his teeth with a toothpick

and then oh didn't you ramble
out of new orleans without the least tribute
without having left a quarter or more

like bix for bessie on a chicago dance floor
where her blues sprouted more tulips
than a gunman's pistol—

> *bessie smith: 1937 car crash*
> *left arm severed near an e.r.*
> *that would not have her*
> *the car seat taking it all in*
> *a red pool by roadside*

anyone care for the photo credit?

awakening

the breath of the heart lingers
on long breezes and split twigs

their bones fracture old trees
that shatter thin as fingers—

there is a road here full of pebbles
bending into stretches of hills

where purple gloves of iris
twist beneath evening leaves

where the round earth rises like a cup
full of silence descending on side streets

all children now at home
rain swells swollen tall thick weeds
leaning into light that slants and fades

angles of wind in the face of a field
of evergreens once pelted with snow—

you were there then in trumpet twilight
dancing a spark in barroom mirrors

music bleeding your lips your
piece held out on a limb

you moved like a scattered fish
scales fluttering the sounds of clouds
in an indignant shade—

the sidewalk around the street corner
fenced like decay

you were either in or out
angling uncertain eyes in all directions

always expecting to reach air
your arms plunged in fear—

now you grieve into a towel like a sieve
first tears then gulps and sighs then laughter
held in the only place you could be—

a charged field putting you on guard
your sight strained through eyelids
that cannot breathe—

jazz cleopatra/black venus
josephine baker in paris

why does baker's backside rock the continents?
why have throngs of men been roused and
even women's jealousy is disarmed?
georges simenon

i wasn't really naked. i simply didn't have any clothes on.
josephine baker

likely where mick got it from

keith thumbing a beat etched in quarter time
a thin man's hips swaying badly to a rhythm
dreaming dance-shaped legs stretched across stages
twisting his eyes slender golden jungle fever
à la betty boop dandridge berry and spike lee

and how that fell out of memory—

paris that suckled each inch of her
beads spotting light-splashed brown breasts
feathers and drums grassy hills and spears
plastic bananas bending a taut waist
sweat taunting twerking thighs

the city claimed her its fantasy
its cocaine absinthe and orgies a ready reply—

fatherless at six two husbands at fifteen
and what she left behind—old houses
cracked roofs and streets brimming coal
stoves and wooden ovens in winter

she cleaned flats hung laundry turned beds
smoke licking windows pillows and sheets
asleep between covers siblings and rats
one beside her mumbling dreams
the others' tails on the nearby dark floor—

thin meals with elbows at table top and sleeves
hovering after over a sink—she left home
to another bed and stove before thirteen—

then twisting her ass down stage mimicking
her legs and laughter held dreams that
took her to dance floors and receptions
openings in philidelphia boston new york

a dressing room with a vanity
the constant knocks and casual men entering
stockings shimmering halfway up her calves
silk-laced black bra dangling open
on shoulders like loose leaves—

and with two rings and after
could she have seen this going in? could she
have known what might occur long before finding

always the same eyes stuck on the same
spaces on her the same smell in the same
places of those whose thirst would never end

who kept their tongues on the make
so many men trapped in her gaze
their hungry hands seeding sheets—

ii
in these shifting segues she saw paris
her body as passage her steps the style
"danse sauvage at the folies-bergère"
la folie du jour wearing sixteen bananas

zouzou princess tam tam la revue nègre
transfixing the site of sex in berlin
conjuring drips and drools she shook

eyelids gathered in twists of blindness
on knees outside studios and salons
with diamond rings and marriage vows—

or strolling the champs-élysées
a leopard leashed "two objects of obsession ..."
amid aching aging white sculptured buildings
playing with skies and passage couverts
by the countless cafes on the grand boulevard—

nights edging out back doors down steps
from stages to daylight in soup kitchens
she touched where hunger bled many
their dry grey tongues wagging disease—

or with picasso hemingway pirandello
rouault le corbusier cummings cocteau wat
the tables at le milandes slipping champagne
oysters chocolates caviar croissants cheeses
bedrooms and bathrooms full of consent
her leopard sitting on a couch
unchained and undisturbed—

then the stretched limbs of the aztec
who opened coatlicue's wolf tongue
and let her raven twirled twin braids fall
a red smile beaming atop nipples—

iii
after there was silence between gazes
until jean-claude marianne janot aiko stellina
noelle kofi brahim luis jari mara moise

took her home to red begonias
green grey foliage scented pink roses
reflecting without blemish in a clear glass pool

aisles stretched into wandering trees with
cockatiels parrots and clear setting skies—

or did she take them to frame her pride
naming each in costume and tongue
siblings by difference exhibited exalted
well-mannered and tamed?
                                                  or were they
walking breaths of what she could never have
their eyes flashing solitude like dim car lights
their lips cut from turmoil and pain

that led her to dance with those whose
words were wrung from viral tongues
sharpened against other eyes—

and she performer "black venus" "l'resistance"
last speaker in washington dc 1963 before king

from silks and gems to debt and friends
princess grace and brigitte bardot
sitting barefoot in rain outside
the chateau that was once her home—

last performance at sixty-nine and three nights later …

from theatre champes-élysées
(1925 la revue nègre first paris performance)

for a short walk to l'église de la madeleine
(funeral procession april 1975 military honours)

and 20,000 cleansing curbstones
with veils shadows and tears

grievance

the spectacle of insolence
despicable loathing and fear—

all day we sit on bar stools
expecting something other
than what can only be

a shallow breath drugged into memory
a tongue that crawled out of mystery
in those moments when we thought

revenge was left on the cracked ledge
of a windowsill behind curtains
and spaces neither imagined nor real—

so speculative the fee we paid
so enormous the vestibule of our need

our legs standing stones
at the corner where we turned
into a side road of emptiness

a vast landscape covering a path
the wide long gates of a horizon

the clutter of bones gripping incest
splints bleeding at the dark edge of midnight

a perpetual anesthetic we interpreted as air
then held our lungs in our throats

like so much seed—

tea for two
for bud powell

under skies huddled between darkness
a brush of leaves on a fence in october
a veil of tears against windows

you sat on a bench without an umbrella
a breath of emptiness amidst small trees
while the bells of cities rang their times

as morning dragged light into shade—

mud then split puddles down empty streets
litter drying rain and newspapers' foreign tongue
street lamps dim in the mist

your fingers once ivory and speed
memory strapped to a table arms and legs
you tried to imagine a home less distant

than how those restraints measured you
after wandering tree-lined avenues
their cold wet grip inside your bones

as you searched for a piano
outside the bland walls of white rooms
wired to electric-shock and insulin

or "managed" in a "glass enclosure"
stripped of everything not stuck to your skin—

your every step a pattern of stories
you could not conceal behind the black
back of a keyboard bar hospital bed

passing out in studios and side streets
a bottle here needle in the other your dream
once grasped then constantly deferred

ii
prodigy challenger master mad
from those times you jumped off cootie's
stages into barrooms staring down art—
tatum and bird—after "hoogie boogie"
and your mother closing doors on "diz"

then returning from a gig
philadelphia to new york
a whisky swagger took you down
delivered courtesy railroad security
their cordiality wearing you thin—

and from that day they held you, what
do you remember? night sticks? elbows?
knees? how many? did they take turns?
were they laughing? were you handcuffed?
was your mouth shut up in a rag?

and who were you in that bar to those
who tied your tongue to their fists? who
sheltered you in blows of shade?

or staggered in the "tombs"? the
guards' grips guiding you? their
fingers like hammers? their breath
a fire of rain? their charge
that left you wondering

was what you were what you
would always be? your body caught
in that space outside of everything
made insolvent with so many nodes

plugged into you so many
sudden vibrations inside a shell

iii
creedmore harlem pilgrim state
bellevue and a philadelphia nursing home
your mind spelled out in letters your
body freezing on deserted streets
upended en route to a local "e.r."—

with william richard mary frances cecilia
june somewhere lost in a memory

each stretch of stays each time you
flew under that zone and returned with
almost nothing of what you once were

plunking down strange eruptions
your fingers wiry and incoherent
your notes fixed with anxiety

that relentless off-beat pounding
of your heart and keys out of time
out of tune out of destiny
with each lamp on the sheets of brilliance
erased like a wrap of vellum in crystal heat

between stockholm paris berlin london new york

the platforms where your piano stood
and where your swift fingers could
no longer hold you nor your old bands—

you fell in and out of halls and bottles
streets curbs benches sidewalks
one or the other you found until
you crawled to the bottom of your liver

forsaking an admiring crew—

iv
but to be what you were every day
had you known would you have done it?
would you have put your throat
beneath that edge of dissonance
only you could hear?

your sound recorded and staged
the hours before and after you stayed
in bedrooms in front of a radio or tv
news sports mysteries and big bands

you mumbling on the telephone
a cigarette extending your lips
ashes powdering trembling hands—

no one knew anymore what you would bring
all your notes were severed and lost
in patterns you would never understand

so that what you let out was not who you were
before they stuck you full of wires and endless jabs
then sent you into a procession of empty streets

until you lay like an untouched key on a hospital bed
with only a few for farewells

until max played you down new york streets
as if it were old school new orleans ...

last song?
for yusef lateef

the yellow trumpet   "big bass drum"
and snare   plugged into sockets—

so many lights   left on their own
the air   stiff with a long note
the pavement   swept with saxophones

as if each held   a moment between
lips pursed   and ready to burn—

it couldn't be just anyone who could take this
who could   sit at the site of the forgiven
and speak without words like a "monk"

(with gifts   offered into hands
full of nails and rope

penetrating the heart   of wonder
sinking like stone   into an inevitable sea)

every sign   pointed this way
every deliberate   sound and spectrum
of light and sorrow   birth and breath

so that even you were astounded   by this seemingly
endless outpouring—

this incredible tension that clings   to your skin—

destination out
for jackie mclean and albert ayler

... then there was this doorway
open and wind blown
with parcels of dust

thrown down narrow halls
as if on speedways, spawning
the silence of pens, and sounds
that fell in dissonance, opposite

shapes and shades, "without
meaning," trembling brittle wind, cold
and unexamined, wounds

softened by healing

the dark forboding
grasp in the metal of lust, of
envy in a source

of loneliness, and longing

hanging like a limb,
on the edge of a rope

dangled, between barrooms
and studios, into it deep
white stuff needling an alto sax

when night set into dawn
and the only agents that appeared
were cornered by red lights

and stop signs—

ii
your nerves breathed bare here
where you thought you were alone
fingers running up and down a register
full of dissociation and despair—

and the audience heard groans
amidst trios and quartets
cigarette smoke and waitresses
hurdling tables and chairs—

masked in silhouettes and solos
the reed hung high in the lips
hot and burning with melody rhythm
gifted graceful with speed—

there was no hiding what ailed you then
this affliction coded in pin pricks on veins
across generations to turn the trick—

iii
plowed into jam sessions,
the rhythm section kicked, whiskey
scotch and soda, storefront
recordings, pressed and labelled
revenues, to almost all—

night light and glasses tinkling
someone with a bottle behind a bar
smoking a half-lit joint
another out back
with powder to feed a frenzy—

what kept the sound afloat
was its own inevitability
its scorched scales searing

the cold breathing bone
usurping its very marrow—

sound its only escape
notes broken beyond, captured
in a space dotted with risk
outside convention, voice

and mystery, holding to, and passing
on a vision, a time lost and remembered
running, thru squawks and squeals—

iv
bells rang, slowly, in familiar
winter air, outside night club walls

newspapers fluttering, across empty streets
tall trees giving way, to a silver passage, stars

and a thin moon, your hat and collar turned
under scarf, black boots pushing against snow—

with each second, reaching into pockets
you awaited some blow, on a street corner

standing next to a convenience store
eyes searching for whirling red lights
ears open to sirens and car doors

and the predictable, a rush of boots
amid shouts, hemming you in—

v
either this, or an episode with madness,
walking down streets, mumbling curses and prayers

shouting at pigeons and invisible demons
waving your mouth piece, as if it were a gift from god—

who else could see your resilient petition
kneeling into such a reluctant abandon

that left you in the grips, of streets
without memory, of boats and steel

your body, hearing only its own calling
no longer open to talk of change—

each pore sensitive to light
in a world down under, sunset

held you like a marionette
dancing in an alter-ego—

what vision then in fields of cold dreams
what woke in the folds of the body

and fell into the ripples of an addict
holding his own, in the mists
of an induced delirium

full of the proxies of regret, sorrow
and a deep blue, fear—

another part

what the music would not tell
spoken by another—you moved
out of clubs at 3 a.m. and fell into
dim-lit old rooms covered in gin—

barrel house bouncing keys
gambling drinks and skins
your sound fell to its own shrill blues
cutting ambiance with speed—

the floor flinging skirts
shoe-tops nylons and pleats
nerve ends filled with substance
you fell out in washrooms
and sheltered down dark alleys

unseen by passers-by
except two with gifts of laughter
six polished objects in an envelope
seeking satisfaction for a transaction
not entirely complete—

they sat close and took your hands
into hands inside black gloves
special delivery one-at-a-time
each making you want
to crawl into a second skin

and lie in dreams that kept you away
from the clenched fists of mercenaries
holding you in places you did not understand

and where they could only take you—

journeying

a long orange crane hangs above a building
like an open claw over grey wind blowing

sunlight clouding evening stars

that guide a lost driver in a volkswagen
to a realm only now dispensed of suffering—

music hovers in this air a choir of chords
in the sky resembles the last day of pain—

paths of knowledge lit by ghosts of separation
these moments end up so surely in any life

of whoever walks alone daring consequences of freedom
like a lone trumpet's fat sound hovering over the ecstatic birth

the end of things

... and having little left to encounter
anything slightly unusual (smoke and doubt
the way the body bends into wind like a tree
rolling over the earth on long avenues of light)
sidewalks storefronts stop signs and night lights
condos restaurants theatres chain stores and boutiques
and everywhere roadside cement steel and wheels—
so little difference in spaces where convenience
hangs on street corners shadowed by buildings
and ashes smouldering the breeze where
clocks came after dripping blood ...

an empty foxhole
filled with fiddleheads

*truly, it is in the darkness that one finds the light,
so when we are in sorrow, then this light is nearest
of all to us.*
meister eckhart

there is a crack, a crack in everything. that's how the light gets in.
leonard cohen

the perpetual ideal is astonishment.
derek walcott

wednesday

it is the geese   in full majesty
crossing the sidewalk   outside the university's doors

such non-chalance   and totally self-absorbed—

all blue in the background   a clear afternoon
students pass them by   ipod headphones out of range

so that   neither of them greet—

a small white paper bag   kicks up in the wind
and a thin blur of cloud   drains the east—

a red car slides forward   thru the designated space
with evening somewhere in the distance   behind trees—

the brown earth bends   into a quick turn at the corner of the road

and it is here   in this idle moment
where frost   comes up out of the tar and slides into the hills—

and it is here   in the breath of several spaces
that everything leaps   into a flurry of wind

and the air becomes home   to shade—

sunday evening

you think of it as a compass
and find relief. when the moon
sits upon the hills
like a mountain goat
you take its direction.

the results were not at all
what you had expected.

coming away from your armchair,
a knot of flesh, with hands
as full as tea cups
and eyes sore with experience,
you see things for what they are
and, for once, are not misguided
or left empty.

you see the roof of leaves
rustle in the easy wind,
fields under gifts of sheep
and women walking on the smooth stones
of night, childless and lonely, under
a sky so arid and heavy blue
it bends over as if an old
man who waits ever so patiently
for the last gunshot of time.

this leaves you standing:
a lone figure, you are a question mark,
a strained memory eluding itself
upon a path so often journeyed
you can never, ever manage
to get lost.

this troubled garden

a blue jay flies from the fence
the black cat crawls to the tree
purple heads of dianthus white
morning glory bells
boston ivy and sweet pea cling
tendrils on the backyard wall—

an airplane splits a ribbon of cloud
green leaves hold up the light blue sky
an old wide maple pencils grey
above a shadowed street—

light in the small corner grocery store
flickers and burns dances and blazes
its doors swinging open with each breeze—

fallen leaves wander into puddles like insects
air bends shoulders
salmon riddle streams
the sky grows fallow like an unwashed sheet
hills rise out of sinking horizons
tall grass a field of wheat
cornstalks encroach the dark
same as memory slipping like a rope
thru the indigent summer breeze—

i then dream myself like no other
lilies trail my blood red eyes
yellow flowering hibiscus steams
the angels' garden gates fly open

as thin dogs marl with rusted teeth
a medallion of birch and rose petals—

a piece of twisted steel

over the roofs of houses   a calm
morning settles   on the green
tips   of leaves
a blue sky, streaked
with white, touches
this stillness   clouds like tongues
lick at whatever   (helicopters,
planes, industrial smoke) moves

a cool breeze emerges   out of grass
rises like a kite   to get caught
or tossed between the limbs   of trees

flies   jump up like jackrabbits
from a food stain on a picnic table
or the fresh scent of dog shit   perched atop
an ill-manicured park   ground
of brown   and green

a church bell   sonorous and solemn
interrupts   the morning silence
on a wrought-iron balcony   figures of sea
nymphs, a piece of twisted steel   not too far
below the ceiling of sky   an old black man
collapses in an armchair his last
breaths bursting like a cannon
from a ledge of reality   a place
where no one   only destiny
can hear   him

while swift young robins flutter
back and forth   and pummel the soil
in a search for worms   and the earth's
elixir   of cool sweet morning dew

circumstance

early light chatters on the lake
geese in formation narrow the site of cloud—

an old white man sitting on a park bench
cyclists and joggers jostling road sides

the waters speak against guard rails
without rhythm.

without strong tides fading into cliffs—

so much depended on so many other things
each embrace an acknowledgement of continuous war

where wind and torch dance with bodies
floating on the crests of unending misery

shadows flat on all surfaces
clutching curbstones against the weight of despair—

pérdida
for lilia leon

beginnings

mama   madre   coatlicue   xochiquetzal

i was drawn here   beside you at this grave site
the brown-spotted broken   stone crucifix worn with age

more dragon now than sorrow

the earth soft and moist   a late morning mist
covering hills   where i've followed my hands and crawled

to that space you set   a tent full of tears

filling me with your memory   of who you were and what
will become of those i love   even though i am far from home

and cannot see them   inside the tongue of my dreams—

yet i see you now   on subways and streetcars
in the cold deep slush   of a treacherous winter

without sandals and piñata   without words
sweeping the air   a knife   suspended on wind

in the folds of your skin   those wounds you buried
into your visions of my days   without corsets apron

and a sunday dress   stitched with bouquets
reds and bright yellows   a child's wear

my bones breathe this sculpture   you fall into my face
and i see through your eyes   and suck the skin

off your every breath—

you are then everything to me   and nothing
an image and a whisper   a tale told through trees

i gather in the half-light   of a february morning—

like memory   ...   re-membering   ...   i remember   ...

abuelita enters

"an old lost woman with no name speaks to me about where i am from ... in the dark night i see her ... planting a cactus ... it reminds me of the sacred jade my ancestors used to take from the earth. plant the seeds and listen to the underground river that feeds your roots."

you are not alone, remember?...

what can i take from this?   clouds of doubt
moments of laughter   your words fill me
madre   woman who holds without touching

my small hands feel your emptiness   your
body lies beneath shadows   like a seed

i speak with your tongue a whetted blade
your sharp cold eyes   soft breasts

i remember their smell   their warmth
i remember soft covers   and folds of sunlight

the gardens where i reached for butterflies

the strings of grey in your dark hair
the earth your spirit walked into these dreams

where i hold you a lover
your smooth quick lips   between my thighs

you keep me warm   with your comings
and goings   you enter me with such delight

that i no longer know who i am

planting the seeds

"mama?!"

they say the wound of love is where the light of wisdom enters
i am in such pain thinking of you   in moments that reach you

have i lost you?   where have you gone?

why are you hiding?   and what offering do you make

in that world where my eyes are closed   and my arms
search for blood in your veins?

mama mi madre grandiose con pelo de azure y oscura

what do i long for?   what song do you sing inside me
like a hummingbird   dancing on my lips?

is it what i fear?   that hushed voice

of the hills you buried   deep in my soul
where coatlicue sleeps   and zapatista orphans sprang

up from rough earth   as if a shaman's seeds

planted next to you   in tents so many men
and women panting in coarse clothes and bitterness

holding rifles in daylight   and knives under their sleep

conflict

"mama! i want more!"

madre me siento tan sola!
mother, i am lonely!

the womb of zapatistas   xochiquetzal
no madre no padre   in care of an "uncle"

the men in rifles and panchos   and the high
hills of fighting   in risk and abandon

your open veins and clogged heart
left you lonely   in the struggle to live on

and take the next breath i take
to speak through my lungs   you breathe

those winds   where i hear coatlicue whisper
your words   and where xochiquetzal

stabs a light   in dim shadows
i then feel the soft red   lips of my openings

now away from a house of birthday cakes   and wishes
a child dancing   in sweet emptiness—

my father ran from you   and held me in his arms against all pain

something you never had   but offer me now
in this cold northern place   that will not speak to you

and is unwilling to let me know   where you are from ...

rape

first i fed the horses   in caves and open fields
water and oats and hay   i brushed and saddled them

and then the goats and cows and pigs
troughs of water scraps of greens

what was left was mine   pieces of corn
bones with shards of meat—

i fought with the men   and camped with them
but could not leave

in my rebozo   carrying my rifle and child
travelling railway cars   bundled in sadness

between camp fires and revolution's beasts
i dressed like a man and ran with them—

refuged in mountains and caves

i was held inside campgrounds   a slave
keeping spaces for them to get enough to feed

my sisters our mothers   myself—

always on lookout   for any who might steal
wood coal stock weapons   me

i slept in darkness with my tent door shut
i rolled in sleep to pretend i was awake—

but then it happened   a knife cut a door
the tent flew open   and he was on me

and i began to kick and bite and scream
and no one seemed to hear me

and he held a knife up to my throat
and tore my belt and vest and pants

and i kicked and bit and screamed
and no one seemed to hear me

and he pulled my pants down my legs
and i felt the cool night breeze on my thighs

with his knife at my throat and his penis
bending at my waist   he began to push into me

he began to push into me he began to push into me

and stayed until the guns of night sounded
an attack   at the west side of our hiding

then he rolled off into his guns and bullet belt
and i found mine

with no more time to kick and bite and scream
with no more time to kick and bite and scream
with no more time to kick and bite and scream

ghost woman

darkness thirst fear voices hills trains
long thin roots shoot through my hair

madre xochiquetzal pérdida coatlicue frida
dry stones cut my bare feet

mujeres volcanos diablo soledad siembra vieja
i look into the mirrors of my hands and hide my face
to see you   ghost woman of my walking dreams

madre   mi madre
on the streets of this city of white stone and cold steel

blackened buildings blocking skies
car wheels and truck horns and sirens

and then i hear a train ...

coatlicue xochiquetzal   inside me feathers
and snake heads flowing hair and a bleeding neck

blood moon sirens gun fire in the night
and you pérdida were you with them?

shedding dresses in that bright night light?

and now where have you gone?   and why are you always
going?   and with you taking my heart?—

you tell me who you were through my blood
and bowels and moon time

in the mouth that smells   these wet openings of arteries
my birth and sex and anger   pleasure and fists

and what i will have   after you disappear
into your bones   and i cannot call or hold you

when i roll into screams of fury   in the rain
of this wintry place   i now call home ...
...
ghost woman, a martyr ... she walks with her breasts uncovered ...
hungry, lost. her full breasts are life. i hear laughter ... and i see death.
i imagine her, a thousand years like this ... my hands remember the
roads that take me home ...

like memory ... re-membering ... i remember ...

the goddess

... a light in the distance ... reminds me of my life, the whole of my emptiness ... my hands remember ...

coatlicue　　　　what did you bring me?
with your snake skirt　　　　necklace of hearts

claws teeth and dagger eyes　　　　a death gaze
you stared at so many

then were held aside by your own until a new birth
drew you under his shade—

xochiquetzal　　　　what offerings flow out of your long hair

where stars hang like bright burning stones　　　　where moons
braid jasmine peonies　　and birds of paradise—

you came to me when i was seven　　a piñata filled with colours
you carried my small brown face and eyes　　my small hands

and yellow pleated dress　　my black socks and endless smile—

whatever i wanted was mine　　　　except what you carried
rivers that ran without end　　destinies encased in shrouds and prayers

my friends laughing in my house　　the songs you did not want
to sing　　　　those memories of hidden gold and jade

the way you invited me　　to join a journey of blood
and there to find you　　　　with a smile red as hibiscus

waiting for an opening　　　　into my as yet undiscovered wound—

the goddess dance

coatlicue   inevitable one
tall as skies   and wide as oceans
twice buried and unearthed   headless
with symbols   on your back and feet

i see you now   through time draped
in a necklace   of hearts and hands
your snake dress   dripping teeth
your shapeless breasts   open wounds

suckling at the lips   of mouths stuck at your nipples
for an ounce of breath   a vein of precious ignorance
like those who placed their gems   around your neck—

you birth all things   heaven and earth
flesh blood and death   the god of sun and war

you rise from beneath the stones of a city
axis mundi sacred temples   from tenochtitlan
you open out to me   and i reach back
a trembling hand   legs thin twigs in brutal winds

i touch your dress   snake heads licking
my fingers fall into their mouths   an awakening

a prayer silence   from your cave beneath mexico city
shattered over skulls and bones   lilacs and red gardenias
i touch your bleeding hearts   and dangling hands
and wander into spaces   left for the dead

without knowing what i am seeking
without thought of how you will greet me
without worry   that your long sleep and hunger
will remake   and swallow me

will feed me poison   give me another name
and show me how to dance   in the heat
with 10,000 drums   and flutes
and revellers   in eagle feathers

and bright spun cloth   clinging
to your bare dripping nipples   that feed all worlds

lilia's dance

and now?   what have i come to? what
do i take?   what is my name?

abuelita warrior ghost woman   xochiquetzal coyolxauhqui coatlicue

you have given your blood   your wombs
your wounds   you have given me the dead you carry

you have opened my legs held me between yours
and i have fallen into your arms   a follower and lover—

your colours burn me   now   like a bonfire
everything i knew and know   all that has led me astray

and into each of your eyes   into the tongues
of rifles snakes visions of conquest   cries of murder

bare asses shattered skulls broken chests and breasts
of women and men   pushing out of my hands my dreams—

how do i hold all this?   within my heart and bowels
my thirst for love and dance   bearing sweet fruit

between my legs   within my breasts
as i am no longer a child   walking through sleep

only to open my eyes   into two spirits
my anguished and uncaptured bones—

my entrails spilling wisdom   beneath my knees
i now know   this new place inside

that says   "i can do what i want, what i dream"
i can love myself ugly in darkness crooked and disfigured

and beautiful   the light and lightning of xochiquetzal

coyolxauhqui coatlicue
who live in me   through those who came before

who remembered   and lost their blood and bones
the ones whose memories   bring me love and light

goddesses of my own journeys and dreams

re-membering   i remember
and my hands remember the road that leads me home ...

vision of the seen

burrowing darkness, stoic figures' red robes, lurking in deluded light, sudden angels, wrapped in absurd, and out of date, ornaments. dangling, on edges of air. a silk permanence, stuck in a web, divinity. trumpets and tongues, like wings. their dull posture, pathetic voice, enclosed against the ever-forward, bending trees. and their leaves, shattering distance, impaled on a stone. on an altar, promising night.

hindsight

it was as if all of your movements were dull
and the light in your eyes fell to your chin—

it was as if   all you saw was a blur of cloud
and all you knew crawled out of its custom
from a large bag of dust and bone—

it was as if each part of you   crumbled
at the moment when night   hovered in leaves

and a red-throated cardinal   sang down the sun
and set the parade of sparkles   into the deep—

it was as if in the mist   so many circles
were absorbed   into an unseemly brilliance

at such deliberate speed each step another destination
so much so   there was little distance thru the structured
dissonance

of waves crashing stones that litter the ocean
with small hills   exploding autumn in the east—

it was clear then why so many throats were dry
their lips   parched with treachery

and how and why
each turned on the other   then themselves

letting nothing remain   in their absence
least of all dignity—

mary
for pam mordecai

i am only known
because of you. you sit
on my left thigh

and your long gold robe
shadows me. i can command
only if you smile.

i can forgive
only if you frown. i can
laugh or cry

only if you speak. i can
share love only in
the shelter of your heart.

each word i breathe
waits a move of your hands.

each wink of my eyes sits in solitude
until you make it real.

this is my tax, my fee, my
penance. i was born from a kiss
and you from the prophets' will.

our fathers alive in backrooms
musing how, brooding at nights,

asleep in solitude with a blanket
and quick hands.

what trials we face telling
these far-flung tales. what doubt
invades our deepest needs.

we belong together. on the right hand
of what is unknowable we are willed:

sexless, petulant, burdened with story
each a puppet to another's dream.

to listen without light

clouds into shelter, their solitude sings, arrows across aisles, a deliberate grace. destination of hardwood, pews splattered with longing, a spray, without warning, you fill this space, alone, no arms or teeth, so caught as you now are, set in a magi's stone, unable to believe, leave. unable to stand in this unspeakable place, this multitude, and its parable. this emptiness and endless fields, absolute nonchalance, without face. without reason.

the order of things

and to have sat in a corner   without breath—
the strain in your chest   all your cavities opened

so that anyone   could ask anything
and you would always say yes—

this was the sequence   you held
like weights   straining your arms
and turning your spine   into stone—

there was no way you could move   even
gesturing   was something to regret—

it was as if   you had come from
some other adventure   and had seen

what could not happen   tomorrow
and all the other things   you would never have

and thereby   they had you
clipped between teeth   like a blade

that cut through   what you were running from—

air burning grass sidewalks red lights and curbs
stacked blocks bidders buyers and sellers

stocks sales skying like a black-winged bull
and everything in your heart facing despair—

you wanted then to sing again   an old refrain
and walk away   from that melody

that strange dirge   of culpability
searing into you   a belt of light—

the passing of light

one view from my balcony leads
to this   a feeling of uncertainty
crows and seagulls gliding into wings
a chain   of buildings mountains
a dark horizon—

a torpor the shape of rain clouds
eases into this   children play
as i once did   in the schoolyard

a man makes his way   by here
i see him   umbrella swinging freely
from his arm   jacket collar
turned up   his step assumes
a faster beat   until they finally
just pick up and run

then fine crystal rain falls swiftly
like thin sheets of ice   perfect
weather for it   the end of june
with workmen putting up
a metal fence to keep
the church across the street
away from its garden

jesus will go lonely this night
caged in with no place to rest
he will not be able to count the flowers
or guess the number of feathers
on a bird's head

others in equal turn will move
alone through this threatening
darkness   even though they may prefer
to wait 'til morning comes

but i have been sitting on this balcony for hours
and am not so sure the sun will rise again

from the sea

discretion

in the pain of light
the discourse as contemptuous as a cloud

in the vertigo of a unique indiscretion
the challenge against all that you say you want to be and are

in the paltry moments that insinuate themselves

in the rusted red agonies hanging like dried reeds

in the aftermath of painted seconds rattled off as if
the blue torpor of a whale's snout exploding wisps and vapour

in week-old entrails stretched across bland skies
at the height of a creeping forecast of disease

in the peculiar moments clamouring of helmeted
construction workers on a sunburnt afternoon

in dizzying winds that clash to hope
or sequins clinging to garments of fear

in endless questions that dodge superstition
and stand on end like a bad somersault

in the cries of wolves seeking affirmation

the incessant chatter of glittering fireflies
and sharp movements seeking reprieve—

stillness

a cool breeze glides like an ocelot
swift and smooth, caressing the shoulders
of passers-by, of readers and lovers

in a coffee shop, children in a sandbox
and thin dogs running thru the park—

a small plane's propellers smack
the light, divide it into unseen particles
of air, sounds that break with music

and instant memories swallowed
beneath centuries of persistent seas—

a cloud hangs as a ball of smoke
in the distance, underneath
a vague noon sun,

hinting rain near land so dry
the hills crack like scabs

weekend spaces

looking out the bedroom window on a saturday
the street below trees, sidewalk lined with impatiens
petunias geraniums, rising beneath the warmth
of an old woman's hand, you see a pace of people

their slow lives made plain, for a moment
without the currency of intimate knowledge
passing, either way as if you and they were
trapped in confessionals dark and lonely

it is mid-july, a maze of heat, still air sitting,
in the window screen and somehow, you see
yourself, at a time when you were wandering,
summer days steaming cool nights, grass rolling
into a dark distance of trees, reptile roads,
slithering corner bends blocking sight, turning
into avenues, empty of wonder

perhaps this is open to sight because of a small boy,
wearing shorts, leisurely pedalling, a shimmering
ten-speed in zig zags, down narrow streets

where you see your own confused days,
when your thoughts were air, in a paper bag
blown up with emotion, each breath
blasting you, into another direction
from what you knew, into what
was a field of electricity
sputtering, in your imagination

retribution

how does one arrive again at birth?

you're given a coin for passage
a boat on a quiet summer afternoon

light glancing over the sure lips of water
you float at the wind's will

then watch stars fall into dawn—

no one ever tells you who is in control
or that anyone for that matter is—

each day is an episode in shadows
nothing in the trees feeds the earth

each crossroad leads to hunger
emptiness in the bowels the spirit leaks—

you are covered then with such misfortune
you suddenly feel you must learn from earlier lives

and where they intersect
with the air you now breathe—

at the edge

let the wind enter   let the sound at the door
step slowly   into the living room

let your lungs   breathe on their own
let your eyes   see what is in and beyond

both cause   and its unknown pedigree—

let the round night   take you thru mist
let its scent   fold into you like a glove—

you will see it then   as anyone might
the difference between   parting the sea to let thru a crowd

and walking on waters   with neither permission nor aid—

alone in one instance   obligation shaping the other
in these spaces   where legacy gives birth

and crawls like veins   across your biceps
and the back of your hands—

and with what you found there   squeezed dry as paper
you carried yourself   into what could only be

from what was
and will always   and always become

something unmentionable   crumbling about you

at each step   landslides cluttering your way
while everything else   rolls down hills—

whispers

the moon now a faint wisp in the cloud-filled sky
whispers cover the sidewalk and fall into the earth

the green-rusted brass bell tomorrow rings into silence
the dull thud of continuing empire claims so many lives

from evening until night time the same expression
captures the ever-receding tree-lined horizon

the leaves of so many oaks maples birch and willow
litter the expanse and bend into endless fields

what shadows the wild tall grass aspires to contain
those bright lights waiting to explode upon the sleeping hills

decisions

palm shade
        mysterious
wisdom
discretion,
flickers
        gentle flame
leaps, fingers glow
miracles   auras
communicate sainthood
        god
        silence
gabriel   armstrong
        trumpet lilies bloom yellow
taking 3 suns   rot grey
        over broken crypt
script   jesus

my voice is little in what clothes i wear
i have no choice in the air i breathe
my voice is little in what food i eat
i have no choice in the water i drink

quan yin   buddha   allah   ramana

i decide only how long i sleep

let the creator take the rest of me

a place to be

soon the peonies will begin to flower—

i want to be there when they bloom
when those big white and red-stippled heads
bend as if in the presence of a bright shadow

such elegance in such deliberate
and contemplative beauty

i want to be there when those large ants
rejoice in their long labour

when the woodpecker stops for a moment
and the hawk slows to admire

when the blades that fall away in to a red-tinged green
gesture ever so slowly on a summer's day—

this is the place to be if only for this moment
a week or so in june every year

a continuum in consistency
where every effort and stretched limb
opens up new ways to see into the deep—

i want to be there when the thin wooden pinnacles
holding the heads of these heavy weights
bend beneath their perfect petals

when the maples' shadows move aside as if in glee—

this thing called time

green ferns bending, like willow. purple petal potato plant glimmering, in sunlight and shade. the black gate, a total eclipse. that moment when the sun, lost in its own gaze, like a plant stuck in a windowpane, the blind lights of mourning, a purposeful place. amid aphids and psychotic roses, roots once in fire, epitome of belligerence, of what waits in catacombs, on hillsides, and the gravesites of the hungry, the damned.

first snow

last leaves lean like cat paws
in the vague dawn, shadows between
clouds, a reminder

of the way we are all
called, without vowels or syllables
symbols of hesitance

or hummingbirds, wings wild
in mid-flight, how long it takes
to balance thin air

on roads stretched like water
clear silver spreading beyond the unknown
a gentle snow at the edge of winter

and chimney smoke hanging in the needled light
its grey slivers slowly a breeze gliding on strings

of whispers—

distance

sometimes it's a simple walk to the corner
past a flower shop and the bookstore that is rarely open—

beside the old wood frames of other stores mending broken furniture
selling drums and stained glass next to an art gallery and a corner
convenience—

with a grey mid-november afternoon's newspapers
tucked in your armpit and your backpack filled with books

you slide behind the long lacquered oak table
at the newly opened coffee shop

dropped in the middle of aspiring homeowners
self-employed consultants lawyers mothers with infants

and the burnt-out bureaucrat crashing in the early afternoon—

the air a hint of coffee an aroma teasingly burnt
you stir slowly the steamed foam atop your cappuccino

settle your fingers into the pages of black print
while a thick ballpoint pen sets your thoughts in ink—

what finds itself as a pattern on paper
bumps against ignorance

what falls like a line of tears
is cradled in birth pangs like a child—

you carried all this unaware in front of you
wandering into so many doorways that opened
tight faucets to reservoirs of need

where whatever moved was hostaged as a sycophant
who was suddenly inconvenienced and ill willed—

letting go

wind swings the evening's   ice-blue sparkling
holiday lights   one way then another

a light rain   falling into place—

angels   view this with abandon
even their counterparts   see it the same—

their every sigh calls itself   the air creaks with sorrow
its waters leak   and we are awash with roses

thin moon and clouds   spread   everywhere
in our faces   always the sense of gloom

without any trail   coming from every direction—

we are then left   wondering
the glow in our eyes   presence of blindness

and its balance   left like wax in our ears—

there was so much   we had let stay on its own
'til each became an encumbrance and something unforeseen

(like a child   suffocating his father in the middle
of the night   a silk pillowcase comforting the way)—

and this is the thread that takes us   the
sudden fall   change in the glance of convenience

on a day when we are left alone
and really cannot fathom   who we were once and are

and how we arrived   at this particular address—

so now nebulous we walk this way

with flashlights   and something to shoot stones—

it is suddenly in our hands   each breath
inside each vein and our faces flush with emptiness

we move into the shell of it   and everything swirls

even tho   all exits and entrances
are filled with other rituals   other jabs in the clouded night—

acknowledgements

my deepest appreciation to Grachan Moncur III and Jackie McLean for the title of this book. it is from their album of the same name that came out on september 30, 1963. this recording has had a profound influence on me both for its deep, soulful and beautiful music and for the way these two worked together.

i'd also like to thank Jim Nason for his careful reading of this work and his generous editorial comments.

i've received grants for this writing from the Toronto Arts Council Literary Program and the Ontario Arts Council Writers' Reserve Program. some of these poems have previously appeared in *Poetry Canada Review*, *Descant*, *Prairie Fire*, *Fiddlehead*, *Revival Magazine* (ireland), *Canadian Ethnic Studies*, *Acta Victoriana* and *Fiery Spirits* (ed. Ayanna Black). *pérdida* was commissioned by Lilia Leon for her one-woman performance. several of these poems have been featured in performances with the *wind in the leaves collective*, which has received both funding and performance support from the Ontario Arts Council, the Toronto Arts Council, the Oakville Centre for the Arts, the 4 Directions Festival, Caminos, Breaking Text (nippising), Blink Gallery (ottawa), the Art Gallery of Mississauga, the University of Toronto Scarborough, the Jackman Humanities Institute and the Arts and Letters Club.

several of these poems have appeared in a chapbook, *whispers*, released in 2014 as part of the Blink Gallery exhibit of Maria Gomez Umana's art, Judith Manger's cello and my voice. these are: *the order of things, the passing of light, discretion, stillness, weekend spaces, retribution, at the edge, whispers, decisions, a place to be.*
i'm particularly indebted to my wife, Bia Rohde, who read these over and over, listened to me read them aloud and supported me throughout the process of creating this book.

"A few years ago charles asked me if I wanted to speak to my grandmothers ... I said yes and together we went on a journey of blood ties, memory and light. I believe the spirits of my grandmothers were eager to be heard, and charles, now my brother, had the love, sensitivity and courage to put their words on the page, while adding the beauty of his poetry to make the messages bright and clear. From our deep bonding and collaboration, *Perdida*, an embodied dance-theatre work about ancestral female wisdom was born."
—Lilia Leon

about the author

PHOTO: Bia Rohde

charles c. smith is a poet, playwright and essayist who has written and edited twelve books. He studied poetry and drama with William Packard, editor of the *New York Quarterly Magazine*, at New York University and Herbert Berghof Studios. He also studied drama at the Frank Silvera Writers' Workshop in Harlem. He won second prize for his play *Last Days for the Desperate* from Black Theatre Canada, has edited three collections of poetry, has four published books of poetry, and his poetry has appeared in numerous journals and magazines.